] Open Interval [

Pitt Poetry Series

Ed Ochester, Editor

] Open Interval [

Lyrae Van Clief-Stefanon

UNIVERSITY OF PITTSBURGH PRESS

Published by the University of Pittsburgh Press, Pittsburgh, Pa., 15260

Copyright © 2009, Lyrae Van Clief-Stefanon

Manufactured in the United States of America

Printed on acid-free paper

10 9 8 7 6 5 4 3 2 1

ISBN 13: 978-0-8229-6036-2

ISBN 10: 0-8229-6036-2

for Justin

. . . and it really didn't have to stop
it just kept on going . . .

Contents

1

For the poor traveler to whom, wild with longing,
Despairing of home, the skies for a moment open
(Mother of God, he says, let them not close)

—*O. B. Hardison Jr.*

Longing, we say, because desire is full
of endless distances

—*Robert Hass*

Bop: The North Star

—Auburn, NY

Polaris sits still in the sky and if I knew
which one it was I could follow it all the way
to Auburn. Oh, Harriet, who did not need the poise
of freedom knocked into your head like sense, who found it more
than possible to sleep, pistol shoved deep into your pocket
along this route, I cannot tell a dipper from Orion.

Yes, the springtime needed you. Many a star was waiting
for your eyes only.

The university twinkles on the hill above my house.
The fat moon rises and a girl holds out her arms. She twirls
in a blue Polly Flinders dress. Mama's precious
cameo—a white woman's silhouette on black satin ribbon
choker tied around her neck. Poise begins here:
in cinders, in rhyme, in splintering beauty into this
and this—: the image at my throat: the summer's pitching
constellations: the ten o'clock scholar's midnight lesson.

Yes, the springtime needed you. Many a star was waiting
for your eyes only.

At the prison at Auburn I cross the yard. Inmates whet tongues against
my body: cement—sculpted—: poised for hate—: pitch
compliments like coins: —(*wade*)— their silver slickening —(*in the water*)—:
uncollected change. A guard asks, *Think they're beautiful? Just wait*
til they're out here stabbing each other. Oh, Harriet, the stars
throw down shanks—: teach the sonnet's a cell—: now try to escape—

Yes, the springtime needed you. Many a star was waiting
for your eyes only.

Icarus

—*for Gus Wing*
who always knew me
when I came home

I hold him together now
Though he is dispersed

The dust in my hands
No one would guess

He was once held
Together by

Imagining
Matisse imagined

The hot red throb
A reachable planet

At a man's center and
All else burned

Away so that against
The sky we saw

Outward inward
The same infinite

Direction
Those stars near us

Exploding their color
Flared like

The yellow feathers of birds
I learned

To fly I learned
To want to fly

From him when he flew and
He fell

The way night will
Always fall

Blue skies straight through
To black

Dear John

A woman writes a letter

One need
Read no further

Your name
The site

To which she won't
Return

I heard *mark*
Used for *mock*

When I was young
Old men sang *quit*

Marking me
Like birds

Swan eagle
Vulture

The summer
Triangle

This was the South
This is the North

And I am
And I was

Astronomical
Parlance

Lyrae I took
To textbooks

I will leave
Here too

But I
Digress

Take you
For example

Reclining Nude, c. 1977, **Romare Bearden**

You want to say she is peach-ripe, fragrant
Dark fruit sweetening around a hard, grooved seed,
The tan parchment beneath her Florida sand
As all things bring you back there—: to land
Your mother's love threatened out of you—: you out of it.
You: a beached thing just made, and open for the sun;
You: a black man's creation—: his simplest collage—: a woman.

There comes a blue that smells like ocean and wet earth, blue
That splits the face's mask and seeps into the eyes.
An evening blue that ghosts you: outlines the hinted constellation
Of yourself: a blue that beads from your pores as you scour
A drenched page searching for form, a man
With sight enough to hang you in the sky.
Hung up, against a wall, in the right light you are

A museum piece: —this wanton: sure as one patch of sea-
Green, a triangle, filtering light between
The curve of your back and the crook of your elbow:
The other, just above your shoulder, the contrast
Of color: —this brown almost defines you: the skin—
You are saved by—layered—paper. Look, the left hand,
Its long, thin fingers, brazen, freeing itself from the body.

The Buffet Dream

In the buffet dream this is what I want—:
Everything I can swallow:
What is hot—: What is cooked—: What is sweet—:
What will fit on my plate—: What will drive me—from sleep
with longing—: This is hunger:—
before the first bite crosses my tongue, waking.

The colors of dream are there at seventeen, each day waking
to promise of silk and open sky—: the gift of truancy: who doesn't want
flutter and slap of wind and parachute, foreign men, falling from Icarus'
    heights? A girl's hunger
for their sweat and the vowels they swallow:
Their neon canopies, their endless drifting, the pull of sleep:—
I could taste everything: the whole of this world: the idea—sweet

as leaving home, as being where I am not *supposed* to be, sweet
as desserts in the dream—: silver bowls of fresh berries and zabaglione:— as
    waking,
just once, to bright lemon tarts with single sprigs of mint someplace where sleep
has wrought miracles. Seventeen—: coarse salt of want
on my tongue, I set out for the territories, hope to swallow
all, at least—: every drop zone I can find—: a black girl on the river Hunger:

—as free as that. I cannot leave this river—: Hunger
snakes along its slumbery route, slow as sweet
syrup, seeks low ground, overflows, swallows
a field, seeps into its green and makes it swampy, waking
the sticky, spongy air, summer's silty edge, wanton,
dripping:—a humid decade's night sweat, a constant of sleep,

until I am in Africa. In Cameroon, *une volontaire*, sleep-
deprived, listening to the dogs scratch hunger
out on Bafoussam's abundant trash piles, I want

the nineteen-year-old boy I snatched like a muddy reed from some sweet
yielding bank, four years back, dreaming satiety, waking,
twenty-eight, purple-mouthed from boxed wine and desire. Swallow

the St. Johns, the Susquehanna, swallow the Maury, the Lom and Djerem,
    swallow
the Atlantic you crossed chasing bright-dyed dandelion seeds to find sleep
a glass display case of napoleons and air-pies, an éclair filled with waking.
Empty-handed on its ever-rocking water bed, hunger
waits you out, weights you. It's possible you've tasted every sweet
nothing your mind can offer, that delicious list you wanted

licked down to nothing, swallowed. Freedom—: the fancy-cakes hunger
designed, decked out in fondant ribbons. Sleep: a night's mouth filled with
    something sweet:—
what each morning, waking, you know you will still want.

Lost

The river, unrolled bolt of silk, gives
evening the smell of fish, wet leaves,
loosening matter. We glide through
its blue-plum tint toward night, the leftover
tang of red wine in our mouths. Upstream
an idea waits for us: if we were lost
how much more would we love each other.
We four move toward this losing with
the steady creak and drip of our rowing.
We cannot in lowering darkness tell direction,
whether the frog's croak came from behind
or before us. Our bellies full, the swamp beckons us
behind its green drapery. Whatever hides
in the tangle—the surprise of cypress knees;
the fierce, sharp-edged palms welting our forearms as
we walk blind through mottled night's
sulfur rot and sucking mud; what flies
into our mouths, impossible to see;
mosquitoes lighting in our ears, their constant
whine high-pitched and crazy-making;
the silent patience of gators and our
wary estimation of their hunger—
we will keep, we are certain, as we lose
ourselves for hours, when we find ourselves again
bank-side, and two must choose to swim because
we're not where we began. The river moves
despite our stillness, our breath
breathing itself into the wet heat, whether
they disappear for good, the two who
splash away, their heavy kicking swallowed by
this evening. I am of the two who wait,
waist high in water, eyes stretched wide to see

nothing but night, washing itself, black
over black in muggy layers inches from
my face, not my hands, skin of water, curve
of meniscus, my breasts where I displace it,
my undissolved legs immersed, merged
with water, losing above, in, out of, but for
these hands sliding over me, another's
hands to keep me from becoming
current tongue, lisp of leaf tips touching
water, but for we, two, touching, agreeing
this is my body. Agreeing, I still belong in it.

Andromeda

because desires do not split themselves up, there is
one desire
touching the many things, and it is continuous
—ROBERT HASS

Someone needs her skin to be white

will make the lie beautiful with words
so it will take

and last, *milk* or *pearl*,
a favorite: *porcelain.*

The lie must not move lest color
bleed in

taint the clean scent of honey, tinge
the white bud. Choose

the opaque stone, the milky
quartz over

smoky, coontail—: if the sun-
bleached crag

she is chained
to makes her skin appear

darker, then call her dusky, a half
lie, a little white

lie. Still, to keep safe,
wrapped in bay leaf, an opal

pressed to her left palm.
See her? A sliver in the polarized

light? A secret
the beach sand keeps, mineral,

earthbound. Gem-
stone hides her: harlequin,

contra luz, gossamer veil,
or flash of fire—:

color a sea serpent's
breath, her bound wrists against

a salt-licked cliff.
Or pinfire—: unconnected

dots of star: in the sky
the thought

of a man makes
a name for herself—:

a galaxy when she opens
her hand, for the boy

knows otherwise:
knows from flesh:

clit from clavicle, the press
of threat and a mirror's

safety—: think of a man and
a man will come:

if he's known enough
of stone her skin

won't petrify him, if
he cannot keep

his own skin from
the truth

then sing *the body
rock he rocks*—: the body:

for marriage: the moorwort's
urn-shaped flowers:

the round black bodies
of notes: their slender black

stems: this
body this body this body

this body

RR Lyrae: Will

When I am dead I may not remember
the mess of purple irises in
the neighbor's garden—or the way I leaned
against their fence to look at him.
Lost to rot, the body:— And the soul?
This is not the time, nor the place.
I will die when it's no longer possible
for this body to show itself best.
It makes me sad, the things I wanted—:
love's gorgeous force:— a tight fat cloud of blue
hydrangea—: someone coaxed the soil to color
] *the universe: — cancer of the hallelu:*— [
my name in his mouth: — an arrogance of vapor—:
a star—: diminished: — sucked down into paper.

Maul

Boy your love's like a tornado
     got me spinning round and round
Boy your love's like a tornado
     got me spinning round and round
It's a shame I don't know sugar
     when or where you'll put me down

You can fry my catfish daddy
     just make sure your oil is hot
Come & fry my catfish daddy
     just make sure the grease is hot
Know I got this side meal ready
     grits a bubblin in the pot

Gone & take that train to Quitman
     Honey leave me if you must
Catch Amtrak to Union Station
     Honey leave me if you must
But just come back for me sugar
     or I'll crumble into dust

I'm a smoke this pack of Pall Malls
     then I'm gonna let you go
Let me smoke this one last Pall Mall
     I'll be good to watch you go
I might set myself on fire
     just to show you so you know

Bout to go dig up some bloodroot
     then I'm gonna shake your hand
Need to slick my palm with bloodroot
     then I'll offer you my hand
When you wake from your sweet slumber
     you be bound to be my man

Boy your heart is like a glacier
        but to hell with all advice
Yes your heart shifts like a glacier
        but to hell with all advice
I'm a stick with you til I fall
        through a crevice in this ice

Come & split my firewood baby
        with your heavy maul
Come on & split my firewood for me
        Honey bring your heavy maul
The way you turn way from me daddy
        It's gon be a hard cold fall

] 2 [

Desire is, among other things, a function
of repetition, or so the very patterns of your life
have led you to believe.

—*John Keene*

your life with its immensity and fear . . .
                    alternately stone in you and star

—*Rainer Maria Rilke*

Penelope

Tropical depression—:
the sky finds the right number and

the tiny hammer in you drops—:
subtler than a click—

as in a clock or combination lock
as the *l* in salt a falling

a pulling down
and in—: you are stitched

to the body—here:
the Atlantic a lust

the wet slap on black streets translates:
even this storm:—

somatic: pulled up from the south
pushed off

the edge of a northern coast
and into itself as rain—:

all day the blue truth—
loose in you

unwinds—:
this hurricane.

Urania's Mirror

> Whoever believes the mirrored world, short-changes
> the world.
> —MONA VAN DUYN

Here,
before your face,
narrative:

its aging players:

the same real God,
the same false, the bull
up there winking,

Aldebaran,
his great red eye,
but you don't see
your wide black eyes
reflected.

Take this compact—:

Hold it up—: Squint
until you recognize
the light—:

It took almost
one hundred fifty years

of charting heaven before
the first celestial cartographer thought
to draw *the night sky*
black—:

You handle these cards with
such care, reserved

for what is rare, precious:
You are not allowed

to bring a pencil,
to touch them;

you must wear white
cotton gloves.

Ithaca

> I'll dig in,
> into my days, having come here to live, not visit.
> —DENISE LEVERTOV

Walking away from it
I think I am this close

to the highway. I am close enough
to see it—and farther—

still

—then—

to hear it. The field—:
shoulder-high grass, wild

flowers— curves me out
of earshot.

One carves a trail

or treks, hikes—skirt
gathered into
balled fists

between her thighs in high grass
in hot weather—the route

already blazed with white
flashes—.

I am not married
to this place.

Some other yes
draws me—the way

train tracks marry
the trail over the inlet

here:—steel, will
over water.

Walking toward—
conflation of

arrival and creation—
making it

—here and
out here where

walking out

to discover anything
but corporeality is bunk—:

I woke this morning—
wed

to the idea
of setting—

copse dampening
what's left of

road noise—

the central narrative
an absence—

carved out—here—
another marker

—a hidden falls
—sound.

Dear John: (Winking Demon)

You are eighteen in November 1782, watching
the sky, as ever, master of a perfect silence, the first
night you note the change and understand—:
You belong to her. And you will lie
stock-still on the rooftop December to May to learn her.

You do not know the sound of your own name
the shape of hers in your mouth. You are patient for
what she will teach each evening she gives you
so little it seems almost less. Tensed for the sensation
you fear: this must be hearing. She turns your whole body
to an ear. Each morning you wake, stiff with listening.

RR Lyrae: Supernova

... eventually.
— JIMI HENDRIX

You love this opening riff— as much as I—
My emptiness— like that of a guitar—
An instrumental hollow—: In the sky
(Where else?)— diminishing's an art—: The star
Explodes toward— invisibility—
] *I thought my life was over and my heart / was broken. Then I moved to Cambridge.* [
                                                    — We
Explode— like this— and Jimi— plays the hurt
Backward— over itself— : The ocean gave
Its miracles—: he sings— : It is enough—
(We watched a documentary—: one wave—
Millennial— at Teahupoo— rose— god-awful
And blue— We saw ourselves— fluid— aluff—)
Whole notes— listing away— from wedded— lawful—

Transit of Venus

The actors mill about the party saying *rhubarb*
because other words do not sound like conversation.
In the kitchen, always, one who's just discovered
beauty, his mouth full of whiskey and strawberries.
He practices the texture of her hair with his tongue;
in her, five billion electrons pop their atoms. *Rhubarb*
in electromagnetic loops, *rhubarb, rhubarb,* the din increases.

Body Worlds 2: In Case

I am preparing myself
preparing to lose—

race—
I don't know what—

 I will do without it—

this

is the most unromantic
way.

I know—:
how to get into

the between,
how to exceed:

divorce, erasure—:

corpses

diligently labeled
plastinate—:

someone's skinned
in-

laws: an exhibition
sold-

out
in advance:

I haven't even seen it
and

I'm
freaked.

⊣⊨

I keep reeling
Kennedy's skull flap—

too pink, shot back

—: the reflexed
hands to

the throat. I'm sitting in

my Element

at the edge
of Cayuga Lake.

It's spring. Why peel it

back, away?
Look

here
at my beautiful

foot—

my windshield's clean.
I rest

my leg against
the heating vents, my

long brown foot foregrounded on
the dash before

the sky's excellent
blue

clear April—
my silver-painted

pedicure. Why move beyond
these

slender bark-brown
silver-tipped toes?—

᳁᳂

What's under my skin?
is ugly:

meat, sinew—? Who

is asking and why ruin
the view

out the window—:
willows, branches

yellow going green,
pushed left of

their shadow-blacked
trunks by wind—

loose and graceful
like the arms of

ballerinas.
Then,

the breeze stiffens: the skinny
strands

straighten, extend

like stick-slim legs—:
arabesque,

en pointe.

Look—:

⚜

no one wants the dead
in toe shoes.

But that's *keeping it real*:
keeping even

the empty body
on display: the real threat

of the exhibition
of seeing

the one who's been posed
holding his own

split skin open—like a flasher—

by its flayed edges.

Clementines

—for my mother

the impulse to save the crate—:

to what end—?   inevitably—

sticky slick of thin and souring juice—

the last gone grey— blue and fuzzing—:

or

alated whip of   sprinklers

blanketing a grove in ice—:

quilt of cold

that melts   will drip itself

to nothing   tomorrow   before—:

inevitably   *oh,*

my darling—:

    or her siblings—

    Joe
    Sal
    Jim

Butch
] *clementine* [
Marion—:

the tart   recipe   Martha Stewart left

one ingredient   out of

so you could not make it right—:

          no histrionics—

ground pecans and an apricot glaze

sliced orange wheels   glistening—:

the history

of seasons of

December   of January—:

                    Jesus

oh Jesus   oh   mother

of God—

what a lady can eat without

soiling her hands—:

Marisol	Oronul	Oroval	Fina
oh	how easily	pulled	from the flesh.

She'll Wait

For the grayest day in September.
Until she remembers the word for
rhododendron, it disappears from her mind,
truant, sometimes months at a time.

For newer words. For a bill
from the cleaning service, the women
who vacuum around her and don't back away
when she jolts awake in the antique bed.

For music, for the rough work
songs, the grunting caesura that separates
daytime from evening, this time from that.
For him to finish rubbing the silk

between his finger and his thumb,
for the fabric to nap. If he wants to dry her
on a white stone in the sun like a plum,
to make something clean and useful

of her body, to make nothing of it,
she'll wait until she remembers
what cannot keep her: Rhododendron:
just yesterday, she did not know the word
for this: Until what's flowing stops itself.

] 3 [

RR Lyrae
stars vary
in
brightness
by radial
pulsations.
As the star
contracts
the surface
heats up
and
brightens;
when it
expands it
cools and
dims. The
mechanism
is the same
in each RR
Lyrae so
the
absolute
magnitude
of each one
is similar
and a
useful tool
for
determining
distances.

Dear John: (Invention)

there in Groningen the body
you wait for me

to give you
and your mother as I

imagine her dealing with
your fever, her faith

the university a heaven of sorts
beyond you glittering

out the window the voice
you release crying

here, Mick Jagger sings "Wild Horses"
there, Banneker carves

his wooden clock, writes his note
to Jefferson *there,*

there, Levina croons, soothing you
silent— the difference

between sound and silence
this lying distance

Penelope

The truth:
There are no suitors—:

I am a black woman alone
In a small town:

One question returns steady
As a breeze roughing

The surface of Cayuga Lake:
Will your husband come home

This week? Neighbors mistake me
For the only other

Black women they've known
They smile—eyes lit with

Recognition—: Not one
Can pronounce

My real name

RR Lyrae: Matter

He still exists as flesh; it's the idea
that's dissipated—: husband :— what was he?
But a word I loved? There is no panacea
for missing syllables: his body: we
all know what matter's mostly made of—: space
obtains—: One day I realized I believe—:
the space in everything is God: that force
of present absence: pen: expanse: I grieve—
] *old fashioned: distance: squinting it into view* [
between body and name— in here! — I'm loose
as love is—: nebulous—: what good
this pointillism—: our eyes won't do—:
Sometimes the absences in us seem so profuse,
I wonder we don't pass through wood.

The Orchard

—*York Springs, PA*

In the orchard
fruit still on the tree,
dark, bruise-red,
undropped.
Fruit not waiting
to drop. The apples
look suspended
as if they might hold
there forever, not one
meant for tasting.
For miles, the trees,
craggy skeletons of a winter,
the apples like painted
antique ornaments,
the backdrop you want
to insult, say grey
drop cloth of a state.
You would not keep
still in this place any more
than you would place
wooden fruit in a bowl
in your living room.
Despite the hills,
despite the road's roll past
the old white house
you thought of purchasing,
for a month wistful
over its tall windows,
high porches, the prospect
of seasons told in fruit stand,
smell of fresh pear, crisp

fall, despite the apples
refusing to fall, you can't
resist leaving here.
You look forward to
the apples. You drive back
just to leave.

RR Lyrae: Sign

Past breath: External: Past gesture: A field—:
the empty space— pressed up between the ends
of fingers and my face— that I extend
out into openness—: a thing I build
against silence— *Dear John:* — This letter penned
in air a self—: in space— a name I find
in your hand—: You : — a listener— a child—
and more than two hundred twenty years—deaf
and dead:— You don't know me from Eve— and yet—
you write me down—: A field—: it stretches out
before us— black— and infinite— and starred
as myth—] *Dear Phillis* [— It does not contain
its ends:— but signs:— the way a name expands—:
I want to say this poem with— my hands.   .

Black Hole

> Poetry exists.
> —C. K. WILLIAMSON

my darkness is not hell
but darkness darkness

is naked and original
is not darkness but

density
and every meaning of in

is before description
compression

is word quark pion
meson atom

is fitting the self into
flesh and aura

a star collapses from
within

itself there exists here
no escape

from slow curvature
winking delay

the crushing need
for form

July 2005, London

⚯

In Regent's Park gardens,
verticality—

spike and explosion—:
green tangerining orange

yellow careening
peach to pink

the upward momentum
of purple—, then

stunning black:—

beauty
of burqa—

a woman:
a walking eclipse.

⚯

She keeps her secret—: a promise—
the terrifying allure of

her body, shaded— her
movement

an almost
silence:—

she *who's*
past— material

whispering air,
quiet as

a peregrine's glide
through snowfall:— the slicing

of a live white
through white.

Blues for Dame Van Winkle

—for Lauren

I drove over to the Catskills
    Met a woman there like me
Took a trip down to the Catskills
    Was a girl there just like me—:
Not so much waitin for her man
    as she was waitin to feel free

M(n)eme

I know a child who believes
he passed through a black hole
when he was born. Talking with him,
I wonder if he somehow remembers
his actual birth. *What was it like?*
I ask him. It doesn't really matter to me
whether imagination or
experience makes his memory.

Once, in Africa, I got so stoned
I time traveled.
I walked into a kitchen to find
I'd entered my mother's life.
It hung about me like a cloud—
her apartment kitchen in the city, the sixties—
visible, almost tangible. The memory
still grips me, leads me by my wrist;
the reefer doesn't make me believe it
any less. How does memory work?
Attached to some mnemonic
it's irresistible: a planet drifts off the list
but for *my very educated mother*
I cannot forget it. Dear
Pluto, I walk this town in search of
you, think I might discover you still
in my neighborhood, behind the P&C,
but no; that's Neptune in the little park,
blue blip held embolic in the thick
glass of its concrete obelisk.
When my mother warned the city
would get into my blood
if I didn't quit returning to it,

was she remembering that kitchen
I visited, apparitional? I smoked myself into her
Manhattan: had she described it
as someplace I would love,
as my father's element, as replete
with poets— I remember: she called them
a bunch of afroed black folk gathered
in a basement chanting I Am Angry —:
How did it get into her blood?

It is there, on the move, in Florida, on
laundry days—: My thirteenth birthday,
I wear the ruby birthstone ring she bought me
from Sears as we hang sheets. I hate
the smell the backyard air will give them. She
hates everything, yet insists this
ritual. She is angry. I wish she'd leave
the laundry to me, leave me to
the itching humidity and crushed
grass, the green plastic basket she
shoves along beneath the line.
Her anger always took her back

to days of wringer washer, scrub board.
She rubbed her knuckles raw against my life,
left me the glint of three hard jewels, red
for love, for July, summer, Cancer, ruby-
red hard knots of blood. She died of
an embolism, a word that also means prayer
and nonsense, whose root means

                                    an intercalation
of days to correct errors—: the ways
we pad the calendar so our year syncs
with the solar year. Here, in Ithaca,
the solar system's laid out on the streets

at one five-billionth scale. Each day
a new transparency overlaying the last,
as though at last it were possible

to slip corrections between: summer's air
stifling, thick with the weight of
                              what can't be
seen: so many thin, clear plastic sheets:
suffocating. And I think of that child
—called John: a name so common as
to also mean anonymous: his name
an event horizon:: how the letters must hold
some speck of memory, some trace
of every previous John imparted
to him—: how can he help but feel
their ever-flattening pull?

] 4 [

O to become a star.
stars seek their own mercy
and sigh the quiet, like gods.

—*Sonia Sanchez*

I too am written,
and at this very moment
someone spells me out.

—*Octavio Paz*

Come Sunday

—for D

Morning was swirling soap bubble rainbow in the eye-shaped space between my
    fingers:
one hard breath and everything would break.

Night had been like that: a risk, the distance
from evening to waking a raised conductor's wand:

the entire orchestra holding its breath,
a rustle of movement settling:
the reed tongued wet, the pattern, whispered

paisley, thinning: an old desire
swept up into his mouth, sent out: a quaver: over shapeless air.

    ❚❚

Picture him now at his prie-dieu: his fingers once knew abalone: the turquoise
    and fuchsia swirl of evening set to make music.

    ❚❚

He seals lament in a box he's lined with pink nipples of packing foam.

He consecrates his tongue and sets
the instrument down, closes the case
on the scent of crushed velvet, cork grease, and saliva.

The trip the light a set of stars throws down
outside his window makes
the last arpeggio.

The meteor shower takes half the night: the fire trucks arrive quietly,
red lights flashing.

Morning was *Come Sunday* in the concert hall.

Morning was this many years away.

Reclining Nude, c. 1977, Romare Bearden

1] Blue

Not turquoise: lithe blessing
curved, heavy lipped,

to tomb, to teach
how shelter devastates;

not our bed, swallowed:
the last memory

in the antique wood
spent, day spent

sweat drowned;
not the ocean

rising

    ] *blue in here* [
thick as a castle wall;

not gorges: Lucifer Falls
carved as though

with a ruler, straight edged,
from the rock—

      bracketed:
the landscape opens: reveals

a mouth wide enough
to walk through:—

penetrable
as] *the body* [

history, penetrable
as song:—

you are my wave—

but wet words; but that

she might take you in—, that
she could divide

herself: accept you:
here: a woman's split

body—:
the spirit

a blue pool just beneath
this existence

2] Blues

] *a neighborhood I am the darkness of* [
I find myself—

between: here:
an ear pressed to] *presto!* [

the ground the sky:—

even over the line
I could hear

her holding her
breath I could hear

her tears I swear
I loved her too—

Oh Durër—
dare

print me
in your planisphere:

I would ink the page
Yes, I possess

all of this

] *blue in here* [

space

RR Lyrae: Magnetic

This is the song everyone
would like to learn: the song
that is irresistible:
—MARGARET ATWOOD

her stillness precedes an idolatry
of motion in his mouth a silver god
keeps wait beneath the spathe of breath she holds
undulant she wants him to speak to say
the god language liquid upon his tongue
to tell her own fluidity the way
seers tell tea leaves floating in the bowl
and reliquary etch upon his walls
some proof of her All longing comes to this
he pierced his tongue so his prayers would be heard
and she wants prayer believes the bright new words
swirling around the tiny sterling globe
his mouth's starred sky their bodies sudden spate
his fluent whispering all that will sate

RR Lyrae: Timepiece

the sun confronts me soloing its light
the sky reclaimed by ordinary morning
a six-piece band of birds begins its tuning
leeching the east of gray what's left of night
elided into day a blue too bright
for me my name an evening allusion
in Magellanic Clouds flickers its fusion
throughout galactic epochs when it's late
the concert hall marquees of heaven lit
with lyrae pulsate flashing in the halos
the ages of a universe in neon
the oldest star's birth date and some have taught
in ancient pinks infinite burning yellows
an infant sun the essence of an eon

Poem for Amadou Diallo

> history
> has taught us much about fame and its
> inevitable tomorrow.
> —LUCILLE CLIFTON

This is your fifteen minutes
of fame. So violently sudden, it caught you
peering at the contents of your life
from outside your Bronx apartment window.
How quickly the vestibule reflects
fame's pop and flare and flash,
echoes with its din—the rapid-fire clap
unexpected as applause.

Your body can't help its poses as four night riders fire like paparazzi,
twisting you with each shot. You are almost dancing—
reaching for what you don't know about America and identity—
your spine shifted, slips. How swiftly you fall. It is impossible to stand.

Your own blood fills your chest until you are nothing but
poems and petals left on Wheeler Street
and your mother's courtroom silence
as she learns to hold her heart.

Ink

... for I have learned,
in whatsoever state I am, therewith
to be content.
—Philippians 4:11

Looking at the inside of
my wrist

I see the tattoo
I am told I cannot

get—: a new shade
of absence

inked
across an old

scar:—sakura blossom,
this snippet

of scripture I want
to flip

into my psyche
daily

with
500 quick flicks—

like checking a watch:
a tick—:

to claim a word
    :content:

I'm willing

to bear the needle
to mar

my skin
with permanence

the artist regrets

will too soon
muddy—: *like looking at*

a painting through
a tinted window—:

so colored
girls may love

color but my skin
can't hold

this vibrancy—:
converts it

instead to its own—

further—:

darkening

Body Worlds 2: X Lady

Her name moves away from her
as if

without the body it could

see the monster
it is. Over there   hung

up like desire
like art on the wall

a black-barred peep show called
consent:—

a form   has been

filled out

but in whose hand?

     If the glove does not fit
you must

forget that

your own middle name's
Niccole—:

I remember how hard it was
to pull myself back

in   by degrees   quickly
like yanking up office blinds

like the sound that makes: accord-
ioned: a ripple

like a countdown to blastoff
like coming but

this

is the violent opposite
of that.

Gender is monstrous:—

her appellation: Lady—
but who wants to sing

this song again?

In from where? —:
from where

I was—: almost

asleep, floating
outside

my body but not

even a German
pseudo-
scientist can find

the space
to which I returned.

I turned a corner

and this is what I saw—

Garden

I too have turned
to the yard

turning the yard
into

frustration of flowers
I have felt for

a knot in the soil
coaxing pulling at

bindweed roots
pulling gently so

they give
half inch by half inch

the vines wound
silently violent

round the necks
of black-eyed

Susans
Name each

flower and the yard
loses

ground becomes
brunnera

bleeding heart bearded
iris

peony purple coneflower
lupine lily

I enter the garden
I enter hackles raised

one finger then two three
sliding into the earth

It falls away from itself
like cake crumbs

If I lower my mouth to it
I can catch the grains

of dirt on my lips
sweep them

away with my tongue

A man who wanted
to tie me to a tree

once licked raw sugar
from my open hand

a policeman he wanted me
to behave

like an animal
From yard to garden

misprision a prisoning
measure   of space

I hold up my hand
and drizzle strikes

at every target
but my palm

I cannot be touched
by anything above me

Blackbody Radiator

A snake shows me
his orange tongue

and I praise him
You—I say—

are beautiful—
to my husband's

absence—
the iridescent black

dragonflies
refusing

my proffered finger
Nothing trusts

how beautiful I can
find almost

anything I must be—
I cross

a field
and crickets leap

away from me
fifty at a time

Blackbody Radiator

I cross a field

and crickets leap away from me
fifty at a time.

Not magic—:
black

disarrangement—:
minutes

before they were music
: swell

and sudden silence—green
grasshoppers scattering

—the ground and I are

shedding ourselves
toward

atmosphere—:
in the movies

a vampire
disintegrates:

in a twinkling
he is

an obelisk of rats
collapsing

running for the door
he is one hundred

bats flying off in
every direction—: his

sexiest trick
is smoke—: he curves

up from the jamb gap
to slip

beneath the coverlets
of a frightened girl

to recompose
himself as music

swells—: a man
above her

in her bed
and something else—:

Dracula's a name for—
our fear of—:

this facility
with which he flies

apart—: pulls her—:

I approach

the smallest of waterfalls for—

splash—:

the way he cannot be held.

Blackbody Radiator

Real objects never behave as full-ideal blackbodies

The radiance or observed intensity is not a function of direction

The net power . . . is the difference between
what someone absorbs from their surroundings
and what they radiate themselves

It will never become invisible
—WIKIPEDIA

We are all called something:
labels

our mothers
affixed to our

new blackbodies
so when we strayed

at least we'd know

to call ourselves:

June:

     Lucille: *Gwendolyn:*   *Eliza-*

beth: *Harry-*

    ette: *Toi:*

   Rita:
      Nikky:

 ] *Phillis—?* [

who's out there

calling you

And what is that

you're

answering
to?

The Ends of Praise

And what is space anyway if not the
body's absence at every given
point?
—Joseph Brodsky

in the consuming dark

    we cannot tell ourselves from

ghosts we are skinless voices

    one says a woman made something

beautiful fall another says slip

    leaves into an envelope

in concert we sound the richest

    black vein through each other

a disconcerting chord a thick fat

    rising Hendrix haunted

his guitar for the ends of

    praise the wheeze of wind

through silk distortion's

    a screaming eagle's memory of

midnight flares from

    the dark's moored barges

we locate ourselves hurting

    for longitude we sink

the knife in powder of sympathy

    and listen to the dogs as they howl

Tandem

You can be in it
and never reach it—

the sky.

I have been—
falling—

for a moment
standing—

one snatched second
yanked

beneath a parachute's
violent

blossoming—:
The sky had no color—

I could not touch it—
It held out

blue as though to hold me
then fell away

at the last second—

I fell

right through right
down to earth

right down

to the drop zone—

to the circle
of pea gravel where

I unbuckled myself from a man
and stood

on my own shaking legs.

"Bop: The North Star": The refrain is taken from Rainer Maria Rilke's first "Duino Elegy," translated by Edward Snow. After the Civil War, Harriet Tubman settled in Auburn, New York. Auburn Correctional Facility, a maximum security men's prison, is located there.

"Andromeda": Harlequin, contra luz, gossamer veil, flash of fire, and pinfire are all types of opal. From the *Oxford English Dictionary:* "A belief formerly associated with the opal was that when carried on the person wrapped in a bay leaf it conferred invisibility."

"RR Lyrae: Will": The italicized words are from the poem "Eternity" by Jasper Bernes.

"Dear John: (Winking Demon)": Astronomer John Goodricke (1764–1786), who lost his hearing in infancy, observed variable stars such as Algol and beta Lyrae from the Treasurer's House near York Minster. His observations laid the groundwork for later astronomers' measurements of the universe. He died of pneumonia at age twenty-two.

"RR Lyrae: Supernova": The italicized portion is from the poem "Vita Nova" by Louise Glück.

The description of RR Lyrae stars at the opening of part 3 is a found poem taken from the Web site http://www.ctio.noao.edu/REU/ctioreu_2001/rudy/ RRLyrae2.html.

"RR Lyrae: Matter": The italicized words are from the poem "Covenant" by Jorie Graham.

"*Reclining Nude*, c. 1977, Romare Bearden" (part 3): The italicized line "*a neighborhood I am the darkness of*" is taken from Jack Gilbert's "That Tenor of Which the Night Birds Are a Vehicle."

"RR Lyrae : Xing": The italicized portion is taken from Linda Bierds' "Rhodolite."

Acknowledgments

The author gratefully acknowledges the editors of the following publications, in which some of these poems, some in different forms, first appeared:

Black Arts Quarterly: "RR Lyrae: Timepiece," "Penelope" (as "Tropical Depression"); *Callaloo*: "*Reclining Nude*, c. 1977, Romare Bearden"; *Gulf Coast*: "RR Lyrae: Will"; *Lit 10*: "Transit of Venus"; *MiPOesias*: "Black Hole," "RR Lyrae: Supernova," "Dear John: (Winking Demon)" (as "Winking Demon"); *Shenandoah*: "Andromeda," "Body Worlds 2: In Case," "Bop: The North Star," "The Buffet Dream," "Dear John: (Invention)," "Icarus," "Lost"; and *Women's Review of Books*: "The Orchard," "She'll Wait".

"Maul" appeared in the anthology *Gathering Ground: A Reader Celebrating Cave Canem's First Decade* (2006).

"Garden" and "Poem for Amadou Diallo" appeared in the anthology *The Ringing Ear: Black Poets Lean South* (2007).

"Garden" was also featured on the Web site *From the Fishhouse* (www .fishousepoems.com).

"Bop: The North Star" was also published as a limited edition broadside designed by Theo Hummer.

"Bop: The North Star," "Black Hole," "The Buffet Dream," "Clementines," "*Reclining Nude*, c. 1977, Romare Bearden," "RR Lyrae: Supernova," "RR Lyrae: Will," and "Transit of Venus" all appeared in the chapbook collaboration with Elizabeth Alexander, *Poems in Conversation and a Conversation* (2008).

Thanks to God for every good and perfect gift. I am grateful to Cornell University for supplemental research and travel funds that supported the writing of this book, and to my generous colleagues in the English department for your support and encouragement. Thanks also to Peter Hingely at the Royal Astronomical Society in London and Martin Lunn, curator of astronomy for York Museums Trust, for information on the stars and John Goodricke. Thanks and a big hug to Dan Beachy-Quick and Ilya Kaminsky, for generously reading early versions of this manuscript in progress and for your valuable feedback. My love and thanks always to the Black Dog Poets (Andrew Allport, Amy Meckler, Rachel Nelson, Rachel Richardson, and Thomas Watson) for this many years of the best idea ever; to my students, who are my kids, my lovelies, my loves, my heart; to Cave Canem, and especially to Nikky Finney for that inspiring conversation on the Hampton Jitney; to Jane and Ron Hicks, for your lovely haven of a home; to Jerry Gabriel and Karen Anderson for your friendship and for so many fabulous dinners; and always, always to Lisa Parker and Robin Puskas, who understand the urge to spin and, whatever about that, it's so fine.